I0085040

Beauty For Ashes

By

O.S. Diamond

Copyright © 2015

O.S. Diamond

All rights reserved. No part of this book may be reproduced in any
form, except for the inclusion of brief quotations in a review, without
permission in writing from the author.

Contact the author at osdiamond7@gmail.com

ISBN-13: 978-0692436462 (Custom)

ISBN-10: 0692436464

Published by

B Clover Publishing LLC

Dedicated to the Author and Finisher of my Faith, those He has blessed me with, and those He allows to enrich my life in ways unimaginable. With all my heart and all my love-

Perpetually, unfeigned-

O. S. Diamond

Barren

Forever is

A mighty, long, time

And our lives are short-

Predictable, at best-

What I feel emulating from your eyes

Is beautiful

This moment

Is as whole as I

Shall ever be

But perfection is flawed

By an illusion

And your perception of how

Much better forever will be

When my only desire

Is right now

My Nature (For M.J.)

Waking up to the realization

I

Had not lived before now

Walking into the world

Its time I take my bow

And I hear him swimming in my head

Lyrics pulling out my soul

There is work that I must get done

Before my time

Is

gone

Submission

I believe we are reading different words with varied meanings

Because what you seem to think the definition of the word to mean

Don't line up with what I believe

And what you are demanding of me

Is not what I was taught to be

It is not about control over a person

It is not about what you can make me do

And you have no right to require of me

That which will not be performed by you as well

So to hell with your self-imposed humanly righteous privilege

As the man of this outfit

Your responsibility of me has nothing to do with my attire

Or those with whom I choose to associate

A personality resided here long

Before in walked you

And she ain't changing because you feel entitled to it

Respect is given as is earned

And much is required to be received

When you can see me as your equal

Then can I trust you to be my head

Unscrupulous

Timelines matters not and

Mean next to nothing to me

I prefer life ergo the rules, any for that matter

When it is wanted is when I want

And if a need is to be met than it must be met

And with urgency

So why should I

Play games

When my p____y likes you,

really

She does

And she is not one to be kept

On any waiting list

Call it what you wish

I call it

As it is

And later just seems to

Take

Too

long

Morning After None

Eyes closed but mind wildly awake

A body stiff and playing possum

Listening to his morning routine

Memorizing the sound of his keys as they jingle

And the fabric of his trousers gliding up basketball player legs

Ending with a snap, a zip, and the tying of

An old leather belt

A cotton top rustles softly as it is pulled

Overhead

Our mini-me follows his movements but

my body dares not to breathe too heavily

Not wanting him to know I'm listening

To his footsteps traveling down carpeted stairs

And today's lunch bag grabbed, the plastic crumpled by his touch

More key jingles and an opened door is softly shut

But my mind's wildly aware

Listening for the chevy's old motor to greet the day

He drives off into the mornings light amidst the traffic

This day holds no morning kiss

He never said goodbye

Snow on the bedroom floor

Ice grows from the ceilings

Lowering the temperature where passion

Once ago ignite

My first love-

of anything-

Whom taught me each

trick I have come to learn

I try to maintain what remains of my balance

Because I don't want to fall into this cold

Infected emotions grow like a moss spreading to

Every awaiting corner

Give me a minute

To catch my breath

Before I am submerged once again

Nothing else can bring me higher

Nor take me down farther than the rapture

Of your manifestation

I can run across a thousand oceans and

Survive solely off the energy that

These intense contradictions hold

That spins me around uncontrollably

Don't Awaken My Love

Don't awaken my love

with the sweetest kisses

planted upon my lips

just to let me know that

you are leaving

forever

don't awaken my love

 with gentle whispers

lightly carried upon your soft breath

just to see what my

 reaction maybe

and do not awaken my love

with reckless passions

that ignite the feral flame

I try hard to contain

just to take the love

I managed to save

because

there is not much more left of me

because once gone

it cannot be replenished

because

I don't want to be left as an empty shell

of the joy I once had

so please,

let her

lie in her comforts

let her

remain in the only safety she knows

don't let ego for a claim take over your judgment-

of you, I beg-

don't awaken my love

Divorce $189

There is just this moment

that too loudly hurts in my ears

For my thoughts to be coherent

If I really heard correctly it would

Have sounded like you were leaving me

But my body went into panic mode

After the parting of your lips and

I could see the excuse for why we weren't working

formed across your mouth

but this old mind of mine screamed too loudly

whose tears are these running

across my eyes?

drowning and robbing squeezed lungs

of breath already baited

yet you stand as cold as this lonesome night in December

contradicting any truth in the professions

your heart previously made

how dare you take me along for a ride

with false pretenses of our destination

yesterday I thought I could believe in you

should I believe the bullets riddling through me, now?

Over and On again

It's been said that someone is always thinking of you

I find it hard to believe that to be true

Somehow I doubt I ever cross your mind

Seems that I'm in this obsession alone

The sole one stuck in the past, oh sorrowful me

It's like a bad song on repeat

The kind you hate but the more it disgusts you

The more it plays in your head

THE LONELIEST NIGHT

Wandering around amnesiac with

No memory of my former self as if

My identity had been stolen and tampered with

My introverted self is the only retreat available

Fighting to find a hiding place from all the concerned *I told you's*

Where can I get an armor of stoic-ism?

To coat the scraps left dangling unprotected

Where my love once grew

His name holds a curse

None dare to speak

A hurt like nothing I've ever heard before

Across my body rages a battle

Of heart versus mind

Discarded promises and empty memories are

Neatly packed away

But familiar tendency won't allow me to keep

The past buried for long

My best was gifted to him

He gave in return indifference

enough to procure a longing

For no other days to be met

So another opportunity to smile again is relinquished

Misery now suits the best

There is only I left

The multitude dwelling within his heart

Breached my level of comfort

And I could not settle for a mere portion

My silent mind longed to scream from

Deceptive dealings so plainly covered

But blackmail proved irrelevant when

Dealing with a contented bunch

All hungering for the addiction that is he

A.S. Glenn

This is my longest wait

the longest line

And still I wait for the promise to appear

From around the convoluted corner

In this unfamiliar territory

someplace I do not

Wish to be

Out in the open with no protection

Wandering behind enemy lines, I am found

But for the promised thing

Of which I remain so sure of

Bravely forward will I forge

Through these tumultuous river waves

Despite my fear of drowning and being over taken

Still on I tread

I seek the face that would inspire the angels

That lingers in the remnants of dreams that hold me

For that face still I wait

and wait

and the possibility of not being able to capture it

with new memories

is enough to murder my sanity.

He, my muse,

whom opened the windows of my soul

When eyes upon him should have been the ultimate sin

Yet I forsake everything else because he has become

Everything else

And yet he does not understand the role he now plays

Christmas Break (Down concrete)

Fickle is a winter love

With its pretenses and deceptions

With its turn-about flippancy

And its cold, cold, heart

The concrete winding stairs

Bearing gifts of pain to bring forth

In the heartless cold

Never let them see you cry

As the frozen stones which are laid upon

A spinning world on its unnatural axis

Bearing loosen grips and unstable high heels

All over and upside down

This loathsome thing called love

An occupant refusing to leave

Taking up a space and dwelling in a place which it

Does not own

Marked full of opinions

 it sits

But no solutions in sight

The cure in lies the cause

But it won't oblige

And why should it

Being a loving thing of pride

And it loves no one for naught.

Daddy's Little Girl Lost

Everyone has a piece of you

 So why is it I still wait in a line

That doesn't exist

Every man becomes a comparison to you

As I search in them for the good qualities you possess

I have been hurt by many

in my wayward past

But their pains had nothing on wounds

You unknowingly inflicted

What is worst?

that my perception only sees

your lack of concern

Or that it deems you the original liar

The first to tell me what I want to hear

Only for your personal gain

Moments that left me hanging onto some unfortunate promises

As empty as the sincerity it was meant to contain

That even at the age I now possess

I still secretly hope you to fulfill

Questioning the continuous love for someone that you

Desperately want to hate

It's like you are two different persons and have me

Feeling two different ways

Once upon a time it was to you I looked

When youth had my mind convinced that you were best

And so many more like me-

With those same old feelings – are forced to learn hard truths

From those who are supposed to protect

The choice was of your own to be the stereotype

But for that choice I was almost a statistic

That left life a disadvantaged fight filled with

Inward demons to struggle with

And a struggle it was

To not be as you

To not allow the lack of accountability -in a presence M.I.A.-

To leave a taste of bitter-ness

But this is your gaping hole

Dwelling within my being

that I tossed anything I could find within it

In hopes that it would close

But it became contaminated by pretty messes

That still I wait for you to help me clean.

Jazz featuring Poetry

Where is my man

See, you don't understand

The seriousness of the current situation

drunk on sounds of blaring horns

tagged by keyboards and drums

and being led by a bass that won't quit

us is stuck inside the minds of something critical

hardcore poets and their poetic rhetoric

entangling the audience members with lyrical

anecdotes conjured with the appeal of something dangerous

life and lust; rhythm and rhymes- stewed into a tantalizing gumbo-

at this interval of space my mind twirls into a fantastic tornado

more inebriated than before

this concoction of verbal alcohol and stimulation quickly unwinds

the tightness of a tensed day

in all honesty we might need to pray, or I may need to pray

 because by happenstance has surmised

an insatiable need to sin

sitting in this dimly lit corner conjuring images of

me and mines through notes flowing effortlessly

from a seasoned sax and its master

he grips her from the back as you would I

fingering her lustrous silhouette and mine eyes

see your hands lacing the flesh of my thighs

turning me on with passion forbidden as if

sneaking a viewing of another's love making session

feeling my own memories of you, my man, in my soul

my pussy remembers you, my man, in my soul

and that stroke you hold burned deep into my subconscious

consciously I escape into us,

breathe in the scent of perfection as we create

 and are replayed

let me put down this devils juice

let me find a shower of refuge from this hormonal possession

this mockery desire so passionately persistent

will not leave me accountable for the impending consequences

I am coerced to express the invasive thoughts that have formulated

So what I need right now is an answer to my question

Originated

 from heated loins

as once more I asked the aforementioned question of

Where is my man.

Not so long ago

It used to be that the sight of me

In your oversized t-shirt would prompt your passion

Because you knew what would not be underneath

It used to be that me stepping out of a steamed shower

Would prompt excitement as you began locking doors

To bend me delicately

It used to be

The clean scents of my bath

Would prompt you to bury your face

Upon my neck and inhale…

Before deliciously tasting my delicacies

It used to be…

But not anymore.

6 Months later

Shower -taking

to make way for violent cries

Tears fall faster than water from the head

Hopes that the sound of the blowing fan

Drowns out the sounds of sobs that escapes

I must hope...

 that God can understand the incoherent moans

that manage to slip amidst

because I can't breathe enough

to get out a prayer

and I can't let anyone see how broken I truly am

this facade has drained whatever it was I had left

my vessel now teeters on depletion

why can I not get out of my head

and run away from what is fast becoming moments past?

Still I sleep…

In his undergarments and oversized tees

Imagining that I am able to catch

Faint remnants of his cologne

We can't be more than five minutes together

Before the urge kicks in

Got me wanting to call him on some

"are you seeing anybody?" mess

Wishing I had the courage to ask him out for a drink

Deep down I am confused, and sure that

My offer of reconnection he would refuse

But still on him I call when in some need

And without hesitation he still comes when I most need it

But this further complexes my thoughts and emotions

And still he is oblivious to my pain

He knows not how it feels …

to see your heart walk away

And know it will never come back

In dreams I call his name

Loud enough for me to awake

Forced into longing something serious

 the comfort of his body warm and sharing our space

missing something serious

his body warm and invading my space

and holding me until I fall asleep

Habitually I tend to forget

where it is we now reside

And it hurts to remember

where we were those evenings past

I can't seem to make my way

through this clutter in my brain

Knowing we can no longer cross

 the bridges of yesterday

A Single Tear

All that I have left to give

All that is inside

To you

A single tear

The last one to fall

from my eyes

My heart is shattered

so there remains nothing to be broken

Now it sits

deep within guarded walls

A discarded

un-treasured

token

Russian Winter

Snowflakes dance on the tongue of

The world

Twirling around the glove

Hibernating trees at full attention

An iced floor birthing a single

Red rose

Friendship lost in the season of death

Unbeknownst to the other pursuit

Summer holds no joyful promise

Winter has robbed me of you

Brighter Sides (so I've been told)

One day I may be able

To see the best in this and

Understand that possibly it was a good thing

But right now I'm pissed

And positivity ain't likely

<u>Speechless</u>

Smeared kisses in a notebook torn

Forlorn pages shredded and

 Marked Upon words

written over and crossed out

Ideas that are crossed again

Looking for the right words-

Still searching

Stokey Green

Stokey green why you

Gotta be so mean

Stop spitting in my water

That water's meant to get me clean

Stop it Stokey Green

Smiling brightly in my face

Laughing at my jokes fooling me

You friendly

Plotting on my space

Eating up my food

Drinking my good spirits up

Getting high on my supply

Leave my cabinets empty

Stokey Green

Stokey Green

Why you gotta be so mean

Spitting in my water

Laughing at my dirt but you

Ain't that clean

Freshly Coifed 11610

The battle has been on going

Many of years

Me

Versus

This hair of mine

Sharing my identity with

The world through my

Semi-precious locks

Time has come for

Our ways to part

To release myself from

Captivity

Of relaxers and destructive chemicals

In this era my freedom depends

On my newest expression

My existence heavily relies upon

This interpretation of the daring kind

So I dare to be

To chop away processed fibers of yesterday

A fresh beginning is today

Meant to be marked down in history and

Relished upon

I embrace my individuality this day

BAMA

Smooth was he in his chocolate skin

 And southern demeanor

Smooth as butter so he was

Never blinked an eye when I asked him

Was she still a factor

And his truths came out as a

Perfect storm

Playing catch with my little tugboat on his

Awesome waves

A "yes" more confident than I anticipated

Tilted me slightly to the left

But the hands were soft

And the lips yet softer

All I could see was him between me

 All I could hear was the imaginary sounds of

Parting knees longing for a pleasure

He had convinced me that only he could prescribe

A subscription that I could not afford but

Loved too much to cancel

Sugary hearts and cartoons blinded my sight and

With a screw you to the world and whomever else he

Left behind in his old one

We built a new one

With his center becoming my galaxy

I let him in,

 Oh my goodness did I let him in

Fear-filled to let him go

Drama and all the exes, currents and in-betweens that he could muster

She did not matter, how she knew

Did not phase what we were growing

Leaving it unspoken between the two of us

And him

She could be his when he returned but

Here he was to be all mine

The Owner of the Blue-Brown eyes

If pain is beauty

Then the world cannot take its eyes off of me

My tears be like paparazzi

Ever present and always at the worst

My emotions are pending a suicide move that

Take me up high in denial and

 send me to plummet deep

down into depression's agonizing abyss

As if I and my tattered heart

are the most amusing things on this earth

And I cannot be mad

Because we are…

Because it's true

My Kind of...

Black rings wrapping black fingers

Black painted nails upon black skin

Wipes tears black with pain held within

Upon a black face with black eyes drained

Staring into bleakness of a blackened life

This is the worst of blackened sight

Void of illumination in this blackened light

With black days and even blacker nights

With black hopes born amidst a black fight

Where black hearts and black minds deterred

Grow into black thoughts from dreams deferred

Black heels black bra black stockings black thongs

Black legs spread and touched by black phalluses long

More black lies drip from wagging black tongues

The promise of colors spoken only until he cums

Black semen raging through black temples

Polluting black bellies raised by one

But Created by two

Another black soul collected in the hell of a blackened Earth

Another black handout, what is it worth

Man I'm so black you can't even see me

And this has NOTHING to do with the pigment of my skin

Or the melanin in my eyes or found in my hair

But of a hurt, a pain so bruised that purple can't find

But a blackness of the soul that once could have out shined

The brightest star in the blackest sky

Something

that could have been anything

A time ago

The kind of black that does not wear off

That does not wipe away

That is never in fashion or

will never get the chance to be pretty

this is hope after life has violated

and not called the next day

it does not get better

it never heals

it has caught a hold of me

   and now

never will i.

There will always be more

He may sleep this night

In my arms, upon my breast

And cover my neck in the sweetest of kisses

My thighs may part but not for sorrow

At least, not upon this night

He may bring a joy more pleasurable than drink

A necessity of strength to take the place of water

But this moment shall be all

In his capacity to promise

Because when this that we have ends

there will always be more

we may connect on ethereal planes

share an essence of supernatural proportions

he may get lost sporadically in my heavenly

and temporarily forget his other engagements

but if I fall into his spirit

or allow him entrance into mine own

if my heart swells from its fill of him

then I must prepare for it to implode

to be torn apart from places deeply within

is the only promised fate I face

for he cannot provide to me that which is not in his possession

when evening has befallen upon our fractured break

and I no longer see with glossed eyes

when adrenalized passions have drained of their fuel

and again I am left to sit, holding an empty bag

so into my world of hurt I will swiftly sink

huddled inside, between walls and floor

the bright city lights will continue beckoning

for his pleasure

when my chapter has been written

there will always be more

Truth of the Undisclosed Matter

He was not supposed to stay

And since she will not leave

This bow will I take

If two should not have been

Then three is the point of intemperance

So this one will remove herself

From the impending situation

I cannot be the coveted cake

While he indulgently eats of her too

And she does not deserve

 to live beneath my comparison

None but him will win if both She and I

remain in love with a stubborn nature

Conclusively determined to outperform the other

Therefore, I speak in humility

 My gift to her the portion I hold of his shared heart

Wearily have I grown of this familiarity

To she of the insatiable thirst

I say drink freely

A Pocket Full of Keys

A pocket full of keys

To doors opened and

Many yet to be

Each with a story told and

To tell

A pocket full of promises

Waiting to be fulfilled

Each with an allure of something better

Before a door I stand

With a dilemma

Urging me to ponder the date I made with indecision

Do I really need *ALL*

Those keys?

<u>Done</u>

There is no

Easier weight to bear

We cannot forget

It can only be regretted

But I will love you

No less…

Notes on A Yellow Pad

His thoughts are that I am beautiful

But I wait for him to change his mind

He gives infinite attention

I wait for him to tire and move along

His pace is gentle and steady

Impatience befriends my lonely mind

Surely he must be blind with infatuation

Me?

. I see reality just fine

His kisses tell a story

Of love beyond the fictional and solid in truth

My kisses hold more worry

Karma has shown Murphy's law does exist

His heart ensures protection

Enforced with strength and care

Mine own hearts is fragile

And looks for him not to appear

Bad Word

You can use many

Descriptive,

Similar, and like words

To cover up

Use in the place of

Or try to make pretty

But there is no way

You can dress up pussy

There just ain't

No way

Agreed Upon Proclamations

Tell me that it's you and I

From here on out

And you got me

No other person will be able to

Overtake what we build

Tell me you

Love me beyond the moment

And you got me

Until I cease

To exist

Reflections

And the day

goes on

with a patience

everlasting

No do-overs

I let go

And we didn't get

Back

But it's ok

From the

bottom of my

heart

I'm happy for you

from deeply within

I

Am happy

Too

There were

Some other plans,

Different than the ones

We made

I believe

To make us see our

Best selves

Yet

Lord know

I have improved

But not because of you

Despite it all

Letting

It go

Was the best thing, yet.

Not So

Oh

You

Silly, Girl

Went and fell in love

You

know

he's been broken and

won't

promise

to be there

has your heart not learned

how many more shattered pieces are you

willing to crumble into

does it somehow get easier

to reassemble the shards

do you no longer sustain cuts

from picking up the glass

of the woman you were

maybe there's something different

only

the

eyes of your soul has seen

and

this

connection

is

not by chance

maybe

you

are

not so silly, after all

Vicious

Legs to the sky

That is what he wants me for

That is what he keeps calling me for

And it makes him angry when I press ignore

And it makes him call me outside of my God-blessed name

But what he got-ain't no different from a million others

And his, don't make him no more special

Ah, but mines…my sweetness has him gone

And my sugar has him crashing

He becomes so drastic to the point of violence

He spews threats to possible contenders, but I only loaned him a taste

I never gave the title

I only promised evening, because I can't give tomorrow

With sunrise and opened eyes to the side on which I slept

Won't find me there

I won't be calling back

My best was given, and with me I take it back

My legs to the sky

Page Difference

Last Saturday night

Inebriated enough to lower inhibitions, I

Uttered the word of those four forbidden letters

In organized deception and

 Ignorant of true happenings

Content in my believing

I said, "I love you"

And, equally

-if not advanced-

In inebriation, to the pinnacle of truth

Acting as a serum

His lips parted with

The utterance of five unexpected words

"I don't feel the same,"

And though strongly influenced with the

Evening's libations

In kicked sobriety

To the stunning revelation

Confused and now futilely attempting to mask

The debilitating blow to an already fragile organ (my heart

and ego)

I became unable to fathom what

Just happened…

But something happened.

Clumsy

I trip over my own heart

But you catch me

Steady me up

That's why I am yours

I can trust you

Count on you

To never

Let me

 fall

Confidence

That is not my issue

Though I pretend

It is not timid-ness

Because I am not

Perhaps a little over the top

So it must be dumbed down

A tendency for overcompensating

The shortcomings of others

And their lack

Don't want to rock the boat

Or intimidate folks

Who could stand to know

The genius that dwells here

So I will keep this ego in check

Rolled up in false insecurity, sincerity, and average-ness

Perhaps slightly megalomaniacal

So narcissistic

What is Seen

To sing a song is not a talent I possess

But I will try to write a poem

As beautiful as you

So when the world hears it

They too can smile

And be in love

You helped to release

What I learned to bury-hide deep inside

The specialness that tend to set me apart

And though I did not wish to stand out from the crowd

You encouraged me to shine

You taught me not to put dimmers on my light

God knew what he was doing

When he crossed our paths

My dearest Friend,

You are a man

Of great beauty

Where Yesterday's Travels Brought us

Into this strange land-

so strangely familiar-

As if the landscape has changed to suit your moods

Sometimes painted in love

But not now

Not today

I sit in hues unknown

In a situation unlearned, unable to properly react

This was not taught to me

And keeping my eyes low-head bowed-

Is the only reaction appeasing to you

But I no longer view the sky

And I seek this peace the heavens taunt before me

But you be the tempest cloud threatening to strike

Me-locked inside, in fear of venturing out into cool meadows and

peaceful variations-

Begin to loathe your existence with a treacherous flame of blue

Burning colder than the heart whose blood your spirit taints

Now I want this gone

His Poetry

Your scent is pretty

I smell your

Beauty upon baited breath

And feel a fire emitted in the smile

That drives me insane

and

Satisfies this insatiable soul

Until I'm in your presence

Of you I cannot

Get enough

Your flow through me is the

Sweetest sentence wrapped in promises that

Emblaze dreams

My memory has become your image's playground

From the moment your light ignited my attention

The ocean's mysteries pale in comparisons

To the grandeur of Heaven's best escape

And I can't wait

To do nothing-with you.

In my own

Before my mirror

I

Stand- all articles of clothing removed

I

Watch

Black nails

Upon long slender brown fingers

Grip and caress

Full

Sized breasts

I

Take in my nakedness

And realized

Just

How

Fucking

 Sexy

I am…

Married

Dinner is on

But there is no him

Homework is done

But there is no him

Kids bathed, fed, resting-to their own quarters

But there is no him

Ohh-here comes that feeling

But there is no him

I guess I'll handle it

But there is no him

Drained, exhausted, my heart aching

But there is no him

I fall asleep to my own tears...

Front door opens

Back door shuts

Storage door opens

Backdoor shuts

Into the shower

Into another bedroom

Guess I'll see him tomorrow…

For the one who is just

For no other reason

Than it being your intentions

Maybe I am growing

Because rather than me try to

Convince you to see it as I

To make it the way I think things should be

I accept the fact that it is

Your will

and ours alone

Slut

Don't stay behind just to appease me

Or relieve some of the guilt you may feel

Because, you want to leave

Because, I want you to leave

There is no need for you to remain

 to try to ease some pain

your conscience served up

In visualizing me, pining over some

 imaginary loss

That's not me

and it won't be today

no reason for you

 to sit down

To stay around

Attempting to forge an elusive bond

As if we were destined to be

It was, what it was

And it is, what it is

There is no pretend

nor pretense

 I'm fine and all

I'm cool with it

Blame it on the right place at the right time

It was my right mind to share that moment

You owe me no apologies

 this is something

I did for me

Yours held no

influence over the decisions I made

Grab your stuff and be on your way

Let me die alone in peace

It is mandatory that I grow

To hate you in order to

get over me…

The Morning After

When the sun is rising

High above our eyes

Overshadowing the trees

Will you still be beside me

When I roll over to my left

Will you be there as was promised

To me

When I am your need

When I reach for your hands

 Will You take me in your arms

And lace the side of my face

With the sweetest kisses you can find

Will you willingly still be mine once

The night passes us by

And we both open our eyes

Adults

Thrown back covers reveal

Missing panties

And mangled bras

Lotions, vibrators, and interchangeable

Batteries

Your boxers stuffed inside my t-shirt

And no clothes to be found upon our persons

The windowsill holds

Empty wine glasses

And chocolate chip cookies

The bathroom smelling of some

Unholy mix

CDs littered

Across the floor

And the sweet sounds of you

Snoring,

passed out, hung over, and et cetera

but we grown now

my have we grown

my how we have grown

Any way I can

I needed salvation

In a pill, a bottle, a dick

Thought I found it in all three

Sometimes together, variations of combinations

Sometimes separate, individually wrapped

But trying to fulfill one longing

Only created another

With absolutely no

Means of escape

And before realized or acknowledged

I had become an addict to something new

In addition to the mess that already had me

So farther I sank

Down a depreciated road

Bypassing any opportunity to

Revaluate my travels

In a flash of proverbial light

I found myself

Not myself

Knocked down to the deepest depths

And even the bottom looked at me

Like when am I going to get up…

The Poem I did not write (Love me some Jilly)

She found the words that eluded me

She said it first and spoke it best

Her pen birthed the emotions I conjured

Her paper shared the stories of my life

And her voice invited the public to the unique experience

I could not hate

Her talent, worthy of yielding the lanes

Alone she stands with high attributes

She accomplished the hidden note

And painted it vividly for the world to view

She sang the lyrics of my heart

And rode the melodies of sacred

Cherished memories

So, at her revelations of my soul

I broke

She took me where I had been

She showed me the moments I did not catch

And missed

She revealed the answers to many perplexing questions

Locked in my head

From prying eyes and convoluted opinions

Our spirits are kindred

Connected in bonds invisible yet strong

She knows all of the secrets

Without ever knowing she had known them...

Fogged

They say

Everything happens

For a reason...

Wouldn't it be nice to

Sometimes

Know what that reason

Is?

Speaking of Misters

Once upon a time we forgot how relief felt

and found ourselves unable to distinguish peace amongst fractured

pieces

dispersed too great a distance for re-assimilation

and they faded into befuddlement

leaving devastation in its wake

so we questioned, if proper relations were forfeited in our contentment

With acquaintances of warped significance?

Maybe the right one was the next one who could not attain his

designation

Due to the occupancy of the wrong one of whom is believed to hold

our elation

Whom was gifted free access to all of our makings

Whom was gifted free access to all of our makings?

Twisted amongst dilapidated soul ties with Mr. Immoral

With trust non-existent this being needs fixin

Aspiring renewal like an enfeebled Christian

And tarry without cease as if waiting for the second coming

The faces of many starts blending as one and invokes confusion

Our kindness taken for being too open

Because they,

Being collective lovers and they

being an assortment of brothers of varying degrees

Twist us head over mind into body

Turn our truth into lies of their choosing and lull us

With bullshit and promises

Snatch up fragile woman-ness under false pretenses

Force us into sexual lethargy

Until we no longer know which dick to trust

Until us don't feel like loving no more

These women without comfort

Unable to stand being held

Because this body only relates intimacy to sex

so if we ain't f**cking why are you touching me?

And faulty thinking has us fooled that it's big pimping

And elevated egos deem us lethal based on his ejaculation

Yet in the minds corner there still sits the tainted visions

Images of what was and should never exist

So here sits we struggling internally

To exorcise demons that were a part of what should not have been

Our naïve selves display our ignorance in the sharing of virtue

with those only possessing a resemblance to

kingdom potential

deemed foolish for not perceiving the vast difference before falling so

freely

We stop loving us to love him more

Now on empty we are distraught

And the past keeps slamming into our doors

Soul ties which were to be abandoned and discarded

Reveal that only we are left to bear

the tainted emblem of scarlet hues

Smelling of lovers old and purity lost

Once upon a time us were unattainable

And then

Surrendering unto capitalized lust

Our name became lost in translation

Bearing meanings that held no association

To the truth beaming in our light

Darkened in a foggy hue of a poisonous perception

Once upon a time we forgot how relief felt

And could not get us back…

Even though we tried

Darker than the Deepest

Nobody warned us

What happens to blue

They never told the truth

Behind the loving façade

Even though they knew

Nobody bothered to share

Those secrets of eve

Hidden beneath the lustrous dark of night

Nobody bothered to tell what happens to blue

The fireworks simply died

With a party's abrupt ending

A passion once readily available

Now determined to give chase

What happens when love turns into uncertainty?

No longer knowing if there is anything left to feel

Yet all along knowing that the

Colors fade

But no one bothered to share

Forced smiles shielded stories that lurked

Behind united fronts of falsified happiness

But there is no happiness

We are not happiness and it seems unfair

We bought into dreams that were for sale

Nobody warned what happens to blue

The truth they never told

Even though it was known

No one ever bothered

To tell what happens to blue

Castes

Read the initiative

Re-read it

Put it down for a bit

Pick it up and read it again

Just to be sure

Damn

And here I was thinking

That we all put our pants on

One

Leg

At

A

time

Unintentional Covenants (that binds)

Here sits I hearing a sermon on soul ties

And feeling ashamed all over

Because here sits I in a purposed covenant yet

Still trying to desperately forget and break those ties

That he, he, and I created when my actions were dictated

By what desires emerged from between my thighs

When enticement was goal achieved to capture sought after attention

But not of enough substance to make him stay

Because I was good enough to have him grant

Whatever I was convinced my heart desired

Now I wish our meeting never happened

I am happy that he left but wish he took

These hellish memories too

I need to rid myself of you, all of you

Yet in the shards of fractured memories

There exists still

Images of him

So confused I struggle internal

To exorcise hell's assignment released into parts of what

Should have never been

With me now harboring feelings as if I am cursed for fleeting

communions because even in the midst of

This new happiness

Torturous shadows of yesterday constantly arises

We on separate roads but still connected by

Distant paths crisscrossed and jotted in history

Refusing to vacate this spot

Leaving me to beg of it to please

relocate with great distance

make this strongman give up this residence

and vacate this premises

but he stuck on occupancy based on the premise

that he got it in first

he won't allow his womb to give another's seed birth

even if that other recognizes my worth

purposing to leave this shell vacant of appreciation

left stuck looking stupid emotional and psychotic

he thinks his seat is reserved

Simultaneous

What are the odds

That we would

Experience

The same

Pain

At the same

time

Coccoon

In a circle of the sweetest smoke

In the sound of the blackest tunes

In the mood of the best emotion

I think I am getting contact

And this Moscato is not doing a thing

But intensifying my senses

I love the times

When I lose me in the

Designer clouds of your sweetest smoke

Mixed with the designer cologne of your favorites scent

mixed with the smell the sweet, sweet smell of you

both of us deep in thoughts, conversation in between

and I sit next to you

 at the table with you

talking to you while thinking of you

glass three still waiting for the buzz I won't feel

until I stand up to leave and you follow me

to our private quarters and we do those private acts

that would make us ashamed if we weren't married

but I get ahead of myself like I so often do

love is now the way your locked hair sway when you lock

into your vibes and zone

head bounce to an 808 rhythm

ears soak in lyrics to feed the soul

I enjoy how you give time to think sort out my ponderings and release

the ink

Amazed at how we connect just being in the others presence.

I don't take a hit but I feel the buzz you search for

I think it's time I put this pen down

And get my fill of you

Wrap my body in your liquid thoughts

As they pour over and between us both

Like the sweet smoke gathering around me

Gather within me

Become my smoke

ENDLESS

i loved to love him

over and over,

 it was love

and music swept over our heads

between our bodies

pressed hard into my orifice

out of my mouth and caressed our ears.

sounds vibrated in waves

to the outside world i became deaf

his eyes burned through me

captured my mind,

my soul's windows-

caught off guard

and lifted-

left unprotected.

he invaded and took domain

rearranging my thoughts

to fit his order

undoing what had been done, to re-do it again

in rapture i drowned

and it was love.

180 days

180 days

180 days of talking

180 days of crying

180 days of writing to cleanse what is soiled inside

180 days of therapy with myself

But if the doctor is sick how effective can

The patient's treatment be?

180 days

180 days of confusion and misleading

180 days of believing and listening

180 days of fighting what I know and

Protecting how I feel

180 days

180 days of recovery

180 days of recovering and slipping back again

Each moment a little farther

Than before

180 days

180 days of he loved me, he told me he loved me,

And loved me so horribly good

180 days

180 days of nonchalant

180 days of getting to me, getting at me

180 days of playing games, me never winning

But I played also

180 days

180 days of back of forth and back

180 days of you leaving checking in just enough to keep hope alive

And me hanging onto you and your words

180 days

180 days of good-byes and talking my heart out of what I am feeling

180 days of purging

180 days of forgetting you touch your smell, your voice

180 days

180 days

180 days

180 days of brave faces smiles laughter

180 days of not knowing

180 days of knowing and not comprehending

180 days of comprehending and not believing

And finally it sinking in

180 days of trying and giving and wishing I could take it all back

And never put it on the market

180 days

180 days of frustration

180 days of rebellion

180 days of renewal

180 days of withdrawal

180 days of coaching

180 days of loneliness

180 days of insecurity

180 days

180 days

180 days in preparation for a lifetime of no you

Scrigglies

He wanted to change me

He wanted me to see in his shade

But I could not change my colors

He drew in spirals, painted in staccatos

But I loved my horizontal lines of straight

Those lines were me

The rationality of my comfort behooved him

And he viewed it as fear

He kept trying to make me see

To make me understand that his different was okay

I am okay

I am difference

I embrace me every moment of allotted breath

But he was not okay with my difference

And me being okay

Made him indifferent

He wanted to change me

I just wanted him.

Today

Riding down this

Road

And it's looking like

A tunnel

With my problems

Overhead

And it really makes me

Wonder…

I cry because I'm tired

Exhausted

Worn too thin and

About to be out

This spirit needs some

Uplifting

As well

Won't somebody rescue me?

Cause I've been saving everyone else

Since the blossoming of breasts

And working for the good of those fallen

Into my care

And I need a break

I need for this to end

My physical is fatigued from

Conjuring

Plans to deliver

Someone else

 Forget about the guidelines let's

Write vacant photos

With fresh frames

Color this wall with dreams

The present stands an unchallenged, uncontested gift

Presented by infallible moments

Gone with the promise of unfathomable tomorrows

Reasoning

She will write by the sunrise

In a darkened room

with nature's rays shining

through turned shades

she will write by the sunrise

trying to push away the world

 with every stroke of letters

her heart released

she will write by the sunrise

in the only moment that she feels alive

unloading what society has heaped upon her

as she taunts back,

" if that was your best-might I suggest

that you keep on trying"

she will write…

For Ashes

I have found a beauty

That the world did not give

So the world

cannot take it away

And even if it tries

And even if it comes close

to prevailing

Yet and still will I smile

Because this beauty comes already protected

About The Author

O. S. Diamond was born in Columbia South Carolina. Artistic expression has been a major part of her development beginning with a love for music that she inherited from her familial unit. As a youth, she would lose herself in reading books and listening to music, quickly realizing the two went together effortlessly in a majestic manner of self-expression. Around the age of twelve, O. S. Diamond began to focus intently on her writings. The author is a proud mother of two beautiful daughters and a handsome son.

www.ingramcontent.com/pod-product-compliance
Lightning Source LLC
Chambersburg PA
CBHW070206060426
42445CB00033B/1612